This book is lovingly dedicated to all those who know that Christmas is not just about the presents under the tree, but about the love we share, the friendships we treasure, and the joy of family gathered close.

May Miss Mylee and Candy Cat remind us all that the greatest gifts are the ones that fill our hearts.

Copyright Sharon Marshall © 2025

ISBN 9781764277617

A Christmas Tale

Every winter, the North Pole comes alive with a flurry of excitement,
this year, there are two new helpers in Santa's magical workshop.
Miss Mylee and Candy Cat, each with their own sparkle and cheer.
Their story is one woven with laughter, mischief, and heartwarming moments,
painting a Christmas unlike any other.

The Arrival at the North Pole

Miss Mylee was not an ordinary Dachshund, she possessed a nose for adventure with her best friend, Candy Cat.

Both lived in a tiny town far away, but it was their big dreams and pure hearts that caught Santa's attention.

One blustery night, a magical letter fluttered to their doorstep.
"Dear Miss Mylee and Candy Cat,
Christmas needs your help!" read the golden script.
Without hesitation, the duo put on their red scarves and followed the shimmering trail left by the letter, which led them to a sleigh waiting just beyond the willow tree.

With a woosh, they soared through the starry sky,

paws and whiskers tingling with excitement,

until the North Pole appeared below.

The reindeer greeted them,

and elves with jingling hats welcomed

them inside the cosy, glowing workshop.

The Workshop Whirlwind

Santa's workshop was a buzz with preparations. Elves zipped about,

wrapping presents, testing toy trains,

and mixing batches of magical reindeer food.

Miss Mylee helped the elves and Candy Cat,

with her delicate paws, was a wrapping wizard.

Ribbons and bows, she could curl a strip of paper into a perfect spiral.

Santa`s Secret Helpers

Though new to the North Pole,

Miss Mylee and Candy Cat soon discovered that

being Santa`s helpers wasn't just about toys and tinsel.

One frosty morning, Santa himself sat them down beside a roaring fire.

"My dear friends," Santa said with a twinkle in his eye,

"Christmas is about more than presents.

Sometimes, the most important gifts aren't the ones wrapped in paper, they're the ones wrapped in love."

Inspired, Miss Mylee and Candy Cat organised a cheer parade for the Elves,

leading them to the "kindness tree," where anyone could hang notes of thanks or a wish for a friend.

The Christmas Eve Adventure

As Christmas Eve drew near.

The sleigh was loaded, the reindeer practiced their leaps,

and Santa double-checked his list.

A sudden snowstorm swept across the North Pole,

burying the sleigh beneath a mountain of snow!

Santa scratched his head, elves scrambled,

and the reindeer huffed anxiously.

All seemed lost, until Miss Mylee sprang into action.

Using her paws, she tunnelled through the snow, carving a path for the sleigh.

Candy Cat, lined the tunnel with glowing Christmas lights,

guiding everyone safely through the storm.

With teamwork and determination,

the sleigh was rescued just in time.

Santa beamed with pride as he harnessed the reindeer,

then turned to his new helpers.

"You've saved Christmas!

Will you ride along and help deliver joy to the world?"

Miss Mylee's tail wagged with excitement,

and Candy Cat twitched her whiskers in delight.

The two hopped into the sleigh beside Santa,

ready for the adventure of a lifetime delivering joy to the world?"

Spreading Joy Across the World

All night long, Miss Mylee and Candy Cat helped

Santa deliver gifts across the world.

Miss Mylee's sharp nose found the right stocking

on even the trickiest mantel,

while Candy Cat slipped through narrow windows with ease,

tucking treasures beside sleeping children.

Every home they visited,

they left not just toys and treats, but a sprinkle of magic.

The Heart of Christmas

When dawn broke over the North Pole,

the sleigh touched down,

and Santa turned to his helpers with gratitude.

"You've shown that Christmas spirit lives in every

corner of the world." Santa said.

And so, every year, when the first snow falls on the

North Pole, listen closely. You might just hear the jingling bells

and cheerful patter of paws,

remember the tale of Miss Mylee and Candy Cat,

and the Christmas they helped save, together.

www.ingramcontent.com/pod-product-compliance
Lightning Source LLC
Chambersburg PA
CBRC101355070526
44583CB00010B/193